IMAGES OF ENGLAND

BISHOP AUCKLAND
TO WEARHEAD

John Dalkin, blacksmith, and his son Joseph at Westgate-in-Weardale.

IMAGES OF ENGLAND

BISHOP AUCKLAND
TO WEARHEAD

TOM HUTCHINSON

The
History
Press

West Blackdene. The newly completed railway bridge on Weardale Extension Railway in 1895.

First published in 1999 by Tempus Publishing
Reprinted 2004, 2008

Reprinted in 2013 by
The History Press
The Mill, Brimscombe Port,
Stroud, Gloucestershire, GL5 2QG
www.thehistorypress.co.uk

British Library Cataloguing in Publication Data.
A catalogue record for this book is available from the British Library.

ISBN 978 0 7524 1525 3

Typesetting and origination by
Tempus Publishing Limited.
Printed and bound in England.

Contents

Acknowledgements

I would like to thank and acknowledge all contributors of pictures, information and photographic services:

Beamish – The North of England Open Air Museum, *The Northern Echo*, Northern Electric, Howden-le-Wear Local History Society, R.A. Alderson, John Askwith (Weardale Railway Society), Keith Belton, Ken Biggs, Brenda Chambers, Celia Dodds (née Emerson), Audrey Fedyczkanicz (née Peacock), Annie Gibson, Ken Graham, Elsie Heeler, Norman Heslop, Mattie Hunter, Harry Jameson Collection, Dorothy Jewitt, Joan McLennan, Margaret Nicholson, Dorothy O'Neill, Joan Potts, Ken Robson, Alan Smith, Stan Turnock, Walter Young.

Special thanks to George Nairn, of Chester-le-Street, for the loan of over eighty postcards and other information, and to Ian S. Carr, of Sunderland, for the railway photographs. Finally, to my wife, Margaret, for her patience and support.

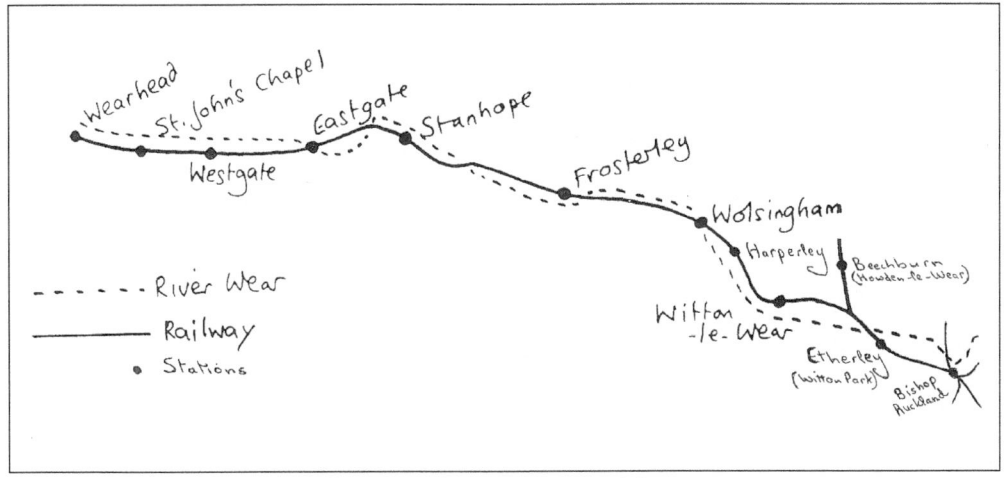

Map showing river, railway and main settlements in Weardale.

Introduction

Early in 1998 I was given the opportunity to work on my first book of photographic material showing the local history and geography of a familiar area. I did not anticipate, of course, the amount of time and effort necessary, but that was more than offset by the kindness of many people in loaning material, particularly, George Nairn, who has 'been down this road before.'

The pictures come from my own postcard collection, family albums, archives and the public collection at Beamish Open Air Museum. They cannot claim to provide a complete picture of Weardale, its people and townships, but will, hopefully, bring back memories of many cherished scenes long gone, but not forgotten.

The book traces the River Wear from above Wearhead to Bishop Auckland as it develops from a young, wild river closely surrounded by the Pennines to the mature, slower moving and winding river we see at Bishop. The railway followed and crossed the river numerous times between Wear Valley Junction, three miles west of Bishop Auckland, and Wearhead. Railway stations and goods facilities were set up along the length of the branch line and we see views of the industrial scene, particularly lead mining. In the last 100 years the towns and villages have changed dramatically, but through the images portrayed, the reader will be able to see places which have long since vanished, and, maybe, recognize people that they knew, or knew, of in days gone by.

Tom Hutchinson
1999

Hill End Farm, c. 1900. This area is now beneath Burnhope reservoir. The Peart brothers are pictured on the left, with Nick Peart's family. Also, in the background, are two girls from Whinsyke (or Whinsike).

Re-opening of Wolsingham Market on 10 June 1904. This market probably originated in the sixteenth century. Miners came to the market for corn, drapery and other wares.

One

The River

Head of the Wear, Wearhead. Burnhope Burn and Killhope Burn join here to form the fledgling River Wear.

Burtree Lynn, Cowshill. There are numerous small waterfalls on the Wear and its tributaries. This one occurs where very hard rock, whinstone, has thrust its way into softer rock formations.

Wear and station from bridge, Wearhead. A young river still, but quite wide at this point. The station was on the south side of the river, the opposite side to the village which is behind and to the left of the photographer.

Bridge End Falls, St John's Chapel. They lie about one mile to the west of the village. There was a footbridge here as well as a ford over the Wear.

Stepping stones, St John's Chapel. The River Wear is quite wide here, but obviously shallow. Two children are pictured, sometime between the two world wars.

Big Falls, Harthope Burn. This burn flows into the Wear at St John's Chapel. There are two series of waterfalls in a valley, which once had a tramway running into it to a ganister quarry.

Waterfall, Slit Woods, Westgate. This is the waterfall on Middlehope Burn, north of the village. The area is covered with natural woodland and there are extensive lead mining relics to be found.

Rookhope. The burn of the same name runs through the village, which is about half a mile north of this spot. This double-arched bridge is on the 'new road' which connects Rookhope with Eastgate.

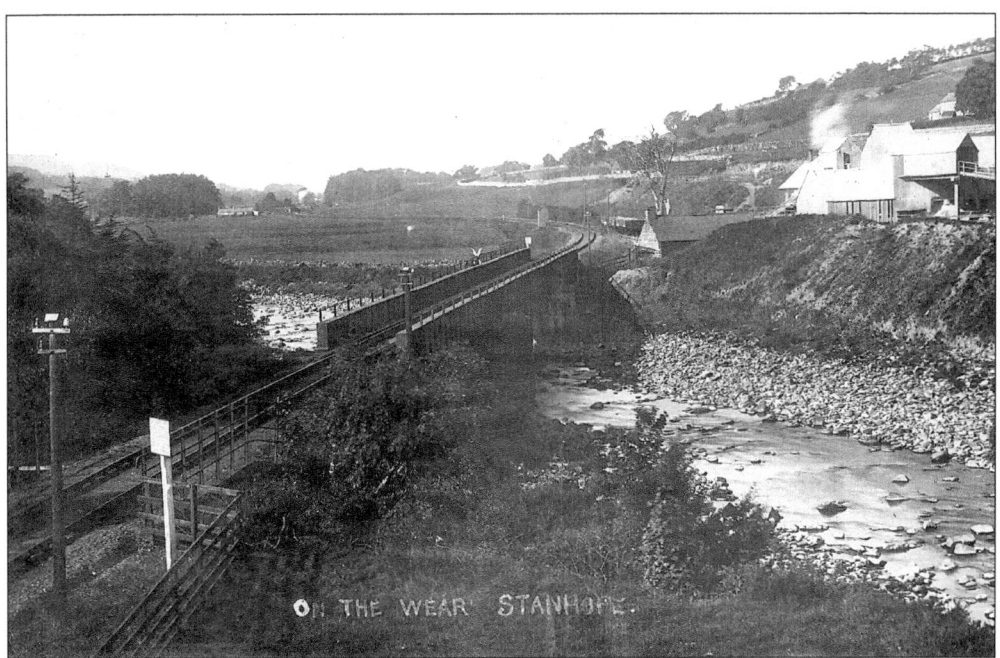

Stanhope. The iron railway bridge crosses the Wear here. On the far side was Summerson's whinstone quarry, at Greenfoot, which had sidings into it from the 1895 extension of the Weardale Railway.

Briggen Winch, Stanhope. This area boasts probably the most scenic stretch of rock and river scenery west of Stanhope. The bridge originally dates from the fifteenth century and was rebuilt in 1792. The deep pool was used for swimming in the summer and skating in winter when it froze over.

Wear Walk, Stanhope. The wall to the right encompasses the grounds of Stanhope Castle. This 1912 postcard shows the much frequented walk along the north bank of the river.

The Suspension Bridge, Stanhope. 5894

Suspension Bridge, Stanhope. Also called the Coronation Bridge, it opened in 1902 to commemorate the Coronation of Edward VII. It was swept away in the bad winter of 1947.

BOLLIHOPE BURN, FROSTERLEY.

Bollihope Burn, Frosterley. The burn joins the Wear from the south-west, about half a mile east of Frosterley. A railway branch along here to Bishopley conveyed more than 25 million tons of limestone and lime during its existence.

Wear View, Frosterley. 4134

Wear View, Frosterley. This is a view of the village across the Wear, with the railway on the far bank. These postcards, with the distinctive style of title and number at the bottom left were produced by the well known firm of Johnston & Son of Gateshead, in their Monarch series.

Frosterley Bridge. 4121

Frosterley Bridge. This is a stone bridge of three arches which stretches over the Wear. It was built in 1814 to replace a temporary wooden bridge that was erected after the original one had been swept away in the great flood of 1771.

The Sills, Wolsingham. This small waterfall is just north of Wolsingham, on the Waskerley Beck. Mr Johnston of Gateshead, the photographer, seemed keen to include people in many of his pictures.

Wolsingham. From here we are looking across the River Wear to the town. The iron bridge was opened in 1893, replacing an old stone bridge which was itself erected after the great flood of 1771.

Witton-le-Wear. It is said that Weardale starts here; below is the Wear valley. The main A68 road from Scotch Corner to Scotland crosses the river on a fine double-arched stone bridge that was built after the flood of 1787.

Linburn Falls. These falls are on a minor tributary of the Wear, which enters the major river just east of Witton Bridge (as seen in the previous picture), not far from Witton Castle.

Witton Park. This shows the two bridges over the Wear, with a train on the Bishop Auckland & Weardale Railway 1843 viaduct, which itself straddles the plate girder road bridge running from Witton Park to Beechburn. The road bridge replaced a ford at this point.

Escomb. The swing bridge over the Wear is pictured, with the young pedestrians carefully posed for the camera. The bridge has long since been removed.

Dam head and weir, Bishop Auckland. Water was channelled off here into waterworks owned by the local district council. Note the salmon boxes that were built to allow the fish to move upstream of the weir. The railway line to Weardale still runs from left to right along the skyline.

Bishop Auckland. The end of our river journey. There are two bridges here over the River Wear; the road bridge built by Bishop Skirlaw around 1400, and the railway bridge on the Durham branch built by the North Eastern Railway in 1857. A road now runs across the railway viaduct, which was closed to rail traffic in 1968.

Two

The Railway

Bishop Auckland Station. A 'panoramic' postcard dating from before the First World War showing (on the right) the east to north curve, with a train for Durham idling at the platform. The platform on the left was the one for Weardale, Crook and Tow Law, in one direction, and Darlington (towards the camera) in the other direction.

Bishop Auckland. A diverted parcel train to Newcastle is about to diverge to the right at Bishop Auckland East in 1960. The Weardale line continues straight ahead while the line to Barnard Castle is in the foreground. The locomotive is A1 Pacific, no. 60132, *Marmion*.

Bishop Auckland. The remains of the old station are pictured in 1986. A train for Saltburn stands at what was the Barnard Castle platform.

Bishop Auckland. Locomotive no. 31319 stands at the current and only platform, with an overnight ballast train, on 6 July 1986. Efforts are being made to complete work on the platform before the arrival of the first passenger train later that morning. The Weardale line is on the left.

Bishop Auckland. Damaged track at Wear Valley Junction resulted in all three passenger trains between Bishop Auckland and Stanhope being replaced by OK buses on Sunday 10 September 1989. The train from Darlington terminated at Bishop Auckland and the bus took over.

Etherley Station – for Witton Park. The train is bound for Crook and Tow Law, pulled by A5 locomotive, no. 69840 in 1955.

Witton Park. Etherley viaduct over the Wear, with the road bridge under the right arch, is pictured in 1988. Compare this with the picture of sixty years earlier on page 19. This was a Sunday passenger service which ran between Darlington and Stanhope.

Beechburn Station, *c*. 1900. We are looking down the gradient to Wear Valley Junction where the Weardale branch diverged up the dale following the river. In this area, at the turn of the century, there were extensive collieries belonging to the North Bitchburn Coal Company, and also brick manufacturers.

Beechburn Station. A view in the opposite direction, looking up the one in forty-four gradient to Crook, which taxed even the most powerful locomotive. The station was named 'Beechburn for Howden-le-Wear' to avoid confusion with other Howdens in the North Eastern Railway's territory.

Witton-le-Wear Station. There was only one platform here with lengthy sidings on the up and down sides used by various mineral companies. The station shown was opened in 1889 as a replacement for the original 1847 station.

Witton-le-Wear, 1992. This shows an Eastgate to Darlington weed-killing train. A crew member of no. 20903, *Alison*, takes the single line tablet from signalman, Ernie Dinsdale.

Harperley Station. The station was built in 1847 with twin platforms and a signal box. It was half a mile from the small hamlet of Low Harperley. No passenger trains stopped here until 1892.

Smash up at Harperley. On 5 July 1901, engine no. 4 of the North Eastern Railway can be seen off the track, behind the locals who have been carefully posed by the photographer from F. Summers of Consett.

Wolsingham Station. Originally it had only a single platform on the far side, but in the 1890s was provided with a second platform that was hewn out of the rocky hillside on the left.

Wolsingham Station. In 1962 locomotive J39 no. 64848 is pictured on a Stanhope to Bishop Auckland goods train. The railway line would have closed completely by the mid-1960s, but for the development of the cement works west of Eastgate which provided enough work for the railway to remain open until 1993.

Broadwood. Between Wolsingham and Frosterley, diesel locomotive no. 47635 crosses the Wear with a Wear Valley Railway party special returning from Stanhope to Darlington on 31 December 1994. Steam locomotive no. 46441 is at the rear of the train.

DARLINGTON, BISHOP AUCKLAND, AND BLACKHILL.

		WEEKDAYS.						SUN.			WEEKDAYS.			SUN
		a.m.	a.m. a.m. a.m.	p.m.	p.m. p.m. p.m		p.m.	a.m. p.m.		Newcastle .... dep	a.m.	a.m. p.m. p.m.	p.m.	SU
...k .... dep	3 45	8 55 7 40 9 57	2 5	3 50 4 55 6 15		9 15	6 35 6 40		Blackhill .... arr	6 22	11 5 12 3 3 55	5 5	6 E
...lington ...... arr	4 47	7 40 8 58 10 55	2 54	4 25 4 49 7 8		9 57	8 12 7 49			7 10	11 55 12 51 3 5		6 E

(timetable, partially legible)

A Saturdays only.   B Wednesdays and Saturdays only.   c Stops on Mondays, Wednesdays and Saturdays only.   d To Tow Law on Wednesdays and Saturdays only.   e Runs between Crook and Tow Law on Mondays, Thursdays and Saturdays only.   On Saturdays leaves Newcastle at 1.27 p.m., and arrives at Blackhill at 2.15 p.m.   Y Steam Autocar.

WEAR VALLEY JUNCTION, STANHOPE AND WEARHEAD.

	WEEKDAYS.	SUNDAYS.		WEEKDAYS.	SUNDAY

(timetable, partially legible)

a Wednesdays and Saturdays only; will commence on 2nd May.   b Via Darlington.   c Arrives at 11.31 a.m. on Tuesday, Thursdays and Fridays during April.   d Via Darlington; on Mondays leaves at 1.38 a.m.

Trains shewn in italics do not run daily throughout the period for which this time table is issued.

Railway timetable. The timetable shows trains both on the Weardale branch and trains to Crook, Tow Law and Blackhill. Until 1935 trains from Weardale and Tow Law combined at Wear Valley Junction for the run to Darlington. It took an hour to travel from Wear Valley Junction to Wearhead.

Frosterley Station. On the north bank of the river there was a good example of the Wear Valley Railway architecture – the original terminus of the railway which reached Frosterley in 1847. On the left is a steamroller with a couple of workers presumably repairing the station approach road outside the Black Bull Inn.

Frosterley Station. By 1989, about sixty years after the previous photograph, the station had become a private house. A rail tour from London St Pancras to Eastgate passes by, led by high speed train no. 43060, *County of Leicestershire*.

Stanhope. Sidings to Newlandside quarries are pictured in the foreground. To the left of centre, on the far side of the River Wear is the original 1862 terminus of the railway, which was in use until 1895 when the extension to Wearhead was completed.

Stanhope 'New' Station. This was built as part of the 1895 extension. It consists of two platforms parallel to the river and is situated on the extreme left of the previous photograph.

Stanhope Station, in the 1930s. From left to right are: Walter Clarkson (porter), A.B. Cundle (station master), Ernie ? (porter) and (on the far left) a little boy running away! Mr Cundle was also the colliery agent.

Stanhope, in 1993. The platform awnings have gone since the time of the previous picture. An inspection saloon can be seen returning from Eastgate to Doncaster, hauled by locomotive no. 31547. Stanhope Station is the headquarters of the Weardale Railway, a heritage railway company, who have re-opened the line between Wolsingham and Stanhope, and hope to re-open the rest of the track down to Bishop Auckland.

Eastgate Station, *c.* 1910. In common with other stations on the 1895 extension, the buildings were of pebble-dashed brick, with wooden ancillary buildings; though the station master's house was rather more substantial. Eastgate was the loading point for ore brought down from Rookhope

Eastgate. Weardale cement works are pictured in 1971. A small diesel hydraulic locomotive shunts wagons that are bound for Newcastle. Now road vehicles transport the products of the cement works through the dale.

Westgate Station. This postcard is one of a series published by William Morley Egglestone before the First World War. Egglestone, born at Huntsfieldford near St John's Chapel in 1838, was the dale's historian and publisher, promoter of the Weardale Extension Railway and a distinguished public servant. The photographer was J.W. Bee of St John's Chapel.

Westgate Station, about fifty years later in 1962. Locomotive class J26, no. 65735 pauses and the West Auckland engine shed crew talk to porter/signalman, Ken Fairless, who worked on the railway in Weardale for forty-one years, twenty-five of them at Westgate. Seated are Ken's father and son.

St John's Chapel Station. A further photograph from J.W. Bee of the railway station, with a posed audience, including the station master – probably Thomas Bates. The station closed to passengers in 1953 and to goods in the late 1960s.

St John's Chapel Station, in 1926 or '27. The two gentlemen are Jack Harbie (left) and Harry Jameson.

St John's Chapel. A rail tour travels up the dale in 1963. Locomotive class B1, no. 61037, *Jairou*, runs round its train while many of the passengers take photographs.

Wearhead Station. This was the terminus of the line and opened on 21 October 1895. It closed to passengers on 29 June 1953 and to goods on 2 January 1961. This would seem a comparatively short life for a railway and station, but, in fact was unsurprising as Weardale lead mining had passed its peak before the extension from Stanhope even opened.

Three

Places

Wearhead, an Egglestone/Tinkler postcard. This is where Killhope Burn and Burnhope Burn join to form the River Wear.

Cowshill in the 1930s. The village straddles the main road from Weardale to Alston. The name derives from the hills where cows were gathered at milking time.

Burnhope town. This hamlet of six farms was submerged beneath Burnhope reservoir in the 1930s. The photographer, Charles F. Tinkler, was a photographer and animal preserver in Stanhope before the First World War.

Wearhead. There is no sign of any cars; just two horses and carts in Front Street.

Wearhead, from the bridge. The Queen's Head public house is in the right foreground, with a small dentist's sign below the lower hotel sign. Perhaps alcohol was considered necessary before visiting the dentist!

The Hills, Ireshopeburn. 11881.

Ireshopeburn, with a view across the Wear valley. In this area were no less than eight ironstone mines owned by the Weardale Steel, Coal & Coke Co. Ltd in the heyday of mining in the 1870s.

Ireshopeburn, in 1913. The post office is on the left and Robert Hodgson, grocer and draper, on the right. This postcard was posted at Cornriggs, Wearhead.

Rookhope. In 1901 Rookhope had a population of 500. The village lies in a beautiful valley just over two miles north of Eastgate. However, there were several lead mines here as well as smelting and crushing mills.

St John's Chapel. The village derives its name from its church – St John the Baptist. Main Street (Hood Street) is seen here in the 1920s, with the Blue Bell public house on the right.

St John's Chapel. The first of two Egglestone series of views of the Market Place. This one shows the King's Head Inn, and the shops to the left that were owned by Dawson & Son who were drapers and grocers as well as running the post office. This postcard was sent at the beginning of the First World War, in August 1914.

St John's Chapel. A second view of the Market Place, to the left of the previous picture, showing the old Commercial Inn (whitewashed) at which, in the days before the railway, the stagecoach stopped.

St John's Chapel. Main Street is seen in the 1960s, with the electricity overhead lines cluttering the view.

St John's Chapel. This is after the removal of the overhead lines by the North Eastern Electricity Board (Northern Electric) in the 1970s, and makes for a more pleasing scene.

Stanhope Market Place, in the 1940s, with the castle in the background. The Pack Horse Inn is on the left and there is a lorry – Jones of Bishop Auckland – selling lemonade.

Stanhope. The Market Place is seen from the opposite direction, with the Pack Horse Inn in the middle of the buildings and the Phoenix Hotel on the left. There was plenty of competition for the railway with all the buses.

Stanhope. The main building shown here in the Market Place was formerly the Stanhope Hotel, and before that the Red Lion. By the time of this picture – the 1940s – shops occupied the site. The cross is a memorial to Stanhope market which died out in the nineteenth century.

Stanhope. The west end of the town is pictured, with the drinking fountain that was erected in 1877 as a memorial to J.J. Roddam.

Stanhope's Front Street, in the 1960s. By this time a combination of parked and moving traffic, on the main A689 road, was starting to cause congestion.

Crawley Side. The steep road up from Stanhope led to lead mines and quarries, and the famous Stanhope & Tyne Railway – the terminus of which was 800 feet above Stanhope. This railway opened in 1834, twenty-eight years before the direct line up Weardale to Stanhope.

Whitfield Brow. This lies about two miles south-west of Frosterley and at an elevation of 1,100 feet. Even here, well above the valley bottom of Bollihope Burn, mining and quarrying was important.

Frosterley. The bridge end or west end, looking towards the nineteenth-century bridge over the Wear. Frosterley was the centre of the limestone quarrying business. The Primitive Methodist school is on the right.

Frosterley. This is the east end, showing part of the green. The postcard was mailed in 1906 and was published by J. Bee, who was originally a watchmaker in the dale.

Frosterley. Front Street, with the local branch of the Stanhope & Weardale Industrial Provident Society Ltd premises prominent.

Wolsingham. The Market Place is pictured, with the Black Bull Hotel on the right, next to the Primitive Methodist chapel. This is the first of four cards of Wolsingham in the A. Johnston of Gateshead 'Monarch' series.

Wolsingham. Front Street, with Whitfield House on the right. The house was a temperance hotel at the turn of the century, run by Mrs Mary Ann Watson.

Wolsingham. The west end of the town, showing a long, gently curving terrace of stone houses.

Wolsingham. The War Memorial, made of Portland stone, was erected in 1920. Each town and village had a war memorial, initially commemorating the dead of the First World War.

Hamsterley. Lying 600 feet above the Wear valley, this is a farming community between the coal mines of south west Durham and the lead mining and quarrying of Weardale.

Mrs Dodds' house, Hamsterley. An unremarkable house perhaps, but associated with an interesting tale which relates that Mrs Dodds was married twice, buried twice, and both her husbands were hung! Her first husband hung himself; her second husband was found guilty of murder after she was buried, exhumed and found to have been poisoned. Mary Jane Dodds was buried by coroner's order on 23 February 1908 in St James churchyard, Hamsterley. Matthew James Dodds was executed at Durham Gaol on 5 August 1908 for the murder of his wife.

Fir Tree. Lying on the north side of the Wear valley, this is less than two miles from Harperley Station and straddles the main A68 road. A small village, it developed at a road junction and was sustained by a coal mine, Fir Tree colliery, during the early twentieth century.

Howden-le-Wear. This community is situated on Beechburn Beck less than two miles before the beck flows into the River Wear. The village developed with the opening of numerous coal mines in the district, as well as brickmaking concerns.

Howden-le-Wear. These are typical terraced houses, built around the turn of the century for miners. The opening of the railway to Crook in 1843 provided the opportunity to develop coal mines around the village, and one pit, North Beechburn, employed 700 men and boys in its heyday. Fireclay was also mined which led to the establishment of brickworks.

Howden-le-Wear. The War Memorial commemorates thirty-three men who lost their lives in the First World War.

Witton-le-Wear. A pleasant view of the village green, with the Wesleyan chapel and school on the right. The village sits on a ridge around the base of which the River Wear sweeps to the west, south and east.

Witton-le-Wear. This view is from the bridge over the Wear, with the railway in the middle distance and the village behind it. The horses plod along steadily and will soon start to climb the bank towards Toft Hill.

Toft Hill. Lying about two miles south of Witton-le-Wear, this is a thin ribbon of a village on the main A68 road. The postcard shows an example about ninety years ago of a great northern institution – the club. In this instance, the Workmen's Club and Institute of Toft Hill and Etherley.

Low Etherley. The original line of the Stockton & Darlington Railway ran underneath this road a few yards from here, on its descent to the Phoenix Pit, Old Etherley.

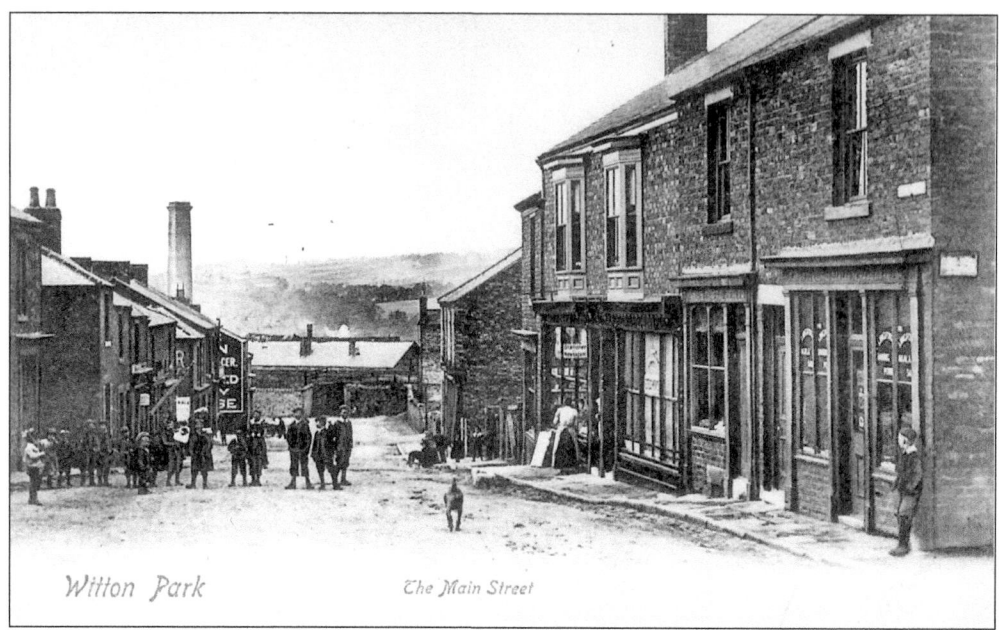

Witton Park   The Main Street

Witton Park. A view looking down Main Street to the ironworks which had closed in 1884. The ironworks had been developed here in 1846 by Bolckow & Vaughan to exploit the local supplies of coal, and also the iron ore and limestone of Weardale which would be brought down by the Weardale Railway. However, forty years later Witton Park ironworks went the way of other inland sites as owners started using cheaper ore from the Cleveland hills, which was suitable for conversion to steel by the Bessemer process. New steelworks then developed at Middlesbrough.

Bishop Auckland. An unusual view from the roof of the town hall, looking westwards along North Bondgate, with the railway viaduct in the background and a train travelling (from right to left) from Durham to Bishop Auckland.

Bishop Auckland. A different view from the town hall, this time looking east over King Street and Auckland Castle and Park.

Bishop Auckland on market day, *c.* 1937. The first bus is advertising a return trip to London for 25s. St Anne's church is on the left and Barrington School, the light building, stands on the right.

Bishop Auckland. Looking towards Station View, the railway station is off to the right. The publisher of the postcard, E. Keen, had his premises just to the right of the horse and cart.

Bishop Auckland. Pictured is Cabin Gate, where there was a toll house in the eighteenth century. The junction of roads to Barnard Castle, Darlington, Weardale (via Etherley) and the town centre lies in the far distance.

Four

People

Bishop Auckland Co-operative Society Ltd. The Committee and Managers in 1903, from left to right, top row: John Peacock (Shildon), Arthur Brown (Close House), Howard Kellett (general manager), John Mansfield (Bishop Auckland), Charles Scurr (Merrington). Middle row: William Hill (Shildon manager), Tom Readshaw (secretary), Alderman William House (president), Fletcher Featherstone (treasurer), James Parkin (Butterknowle manager). Bottom row: William Liddle (Butterknowle & Evenwood), George Robinson (New Shildon), John Rogerson (Spennymoor manager), Joseph Elliott (Spennymoor), William Heslop (High Grange).

Bishop Auckland. King James I Grammar School football team in 1913/14, outside the headmaster's house. Robert Bousfield was probably the headmaster at the time.

Bishop Auckland. King James I Grammar School senior football team are pictured in 1936/37. Andrew Morrison is the headmaster, sitting at the front, in the middle. Les Rawe, who became the physical education master (from 1954 to 1961), sits at the front right.

Bishop Auckland. The cycle club is pictured at Croft Spa in 1907. The gentleman sitting at the front left (smoking a cigarette) is John Porritt.

Bishop Auckland. The cycle club, once again at Croft Spa. The group is mixed this time and includes Violet and May Porritt along with John Porritt.

Bishop Auckland. Pictured at St Anne's Infant School in 1949, from left to right, back row: Terry Barker, Gordon Rutherford, John Ogilvy, Harry Coglan. Middle row: Barbara Brown, Alan Hall, Tommy Hutchinson, Colin Gregg, David Leighton, Gerald Tipling, Albert Hawkes, -?-, Brenda Hutchinson. Front row: Eileen Coglan, Sandra Scaife, Joan Stocks, Marion Soulsby, -?-, Loretta Norman, Josephine Weatherburn, -?-, Eileen Fitzgerald, -?-, Norma Jackson, Pauline Mudd. Seated on the floor: -?-, Harold Briggs, Billy Mounsey, Freddy Clayton.

Bishop Auckland. This postcard, dated 25 July 1907, shows a mostly youthful audience clustered round a pony pulling a tub of coal from Newton Cap Colliery in a procession, which had occurred on the previous Saturday according to the message on the reverse. Newton Cap Colliery was sunk in 1859, closed around 1930, then opened again from 1937 to 1967.

Bishop Auckland. Wear Valley Rovers were a local team around 1930 who played on a field adjacent to Vinovia Roman fort. I remember that field being full of turnips years later! Pictured from left to right, back row: Martin Hunt, George Roddam, Joseph Saunders, -?-, -?-, John Fletcher. Front row: ? Jackson, -?-, ? Davis, Billy Morris, -?-.

Toronto. About one hundred years ago we see Frances Hughes, farm labourer, posing with a rather vicious looking scythe at a farm on the north bank of the Wear, near Toronto.

KINGS BISHOP AUCKLAND.

One week only, commencing Jan. 8

Douglas Fairbanks in

THE THREE MUSKETEERS

Assisted Thursday, Friday and Saturday, by

George Walsh in
DYNAMITE ALLEN

LOOK OUT FOR
"WAY DOWN EAST"
and CHARLIE CHAPLIN

Entertainment. In the 1920s the cinema was the place to go. *The Three Musketeers*, starring Douglas Fairbanks was released in 1921 and this postcard was advertising the film in January 1922 or 1923. The Kings Hall Cinema in Newgate Street opened in 1913 and closed about fifty years later.

JOLLY GOOD BEER AT BISHOP AUCKLAND

Entertainment of a different sort! A comic card advertises jolly good beer at Bishop Auckland, which 'boasted' 32 inns, hotels and taverns, 14 beer houses and 2 brewers in 1856; there were 6 hotels and over 40 inns and public houses by 1906.

Etherley School Class. George Nicholson (middle row, second from right) achieved 406 out of 416 in his exams in 1902.

Etherley School. This is the music class in 1901. George Nicholson is the boy sitting down at the front right.

Witton Park Athletic FC. They were the winners of the Wear Valley League in 1902/3.

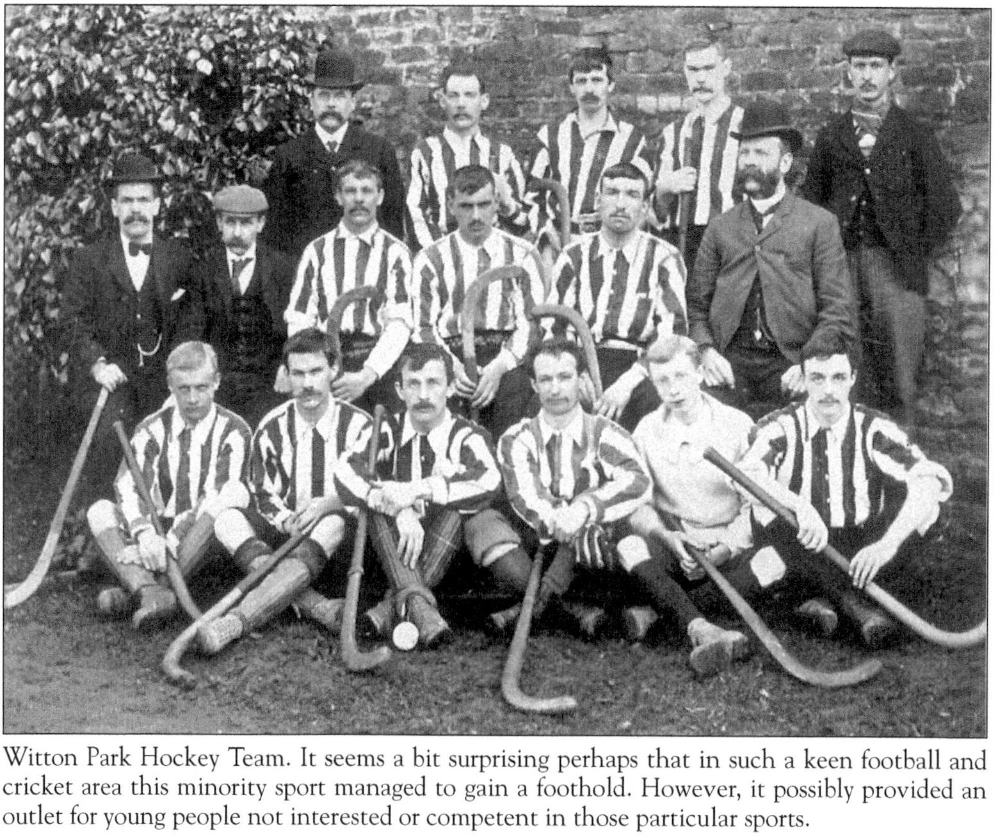

Witton Park Hockey Team. It seems a bit surprising perhaps that in such a keen football and cricket area this minority sport managed to gain a foothold. However, it possibly provided an outlet for young people not interested or competent in those particular sports.

Witton Park. Peace celebrations take place at Woodside in 1918. The band has stopped marching so that the photographer can get them in focus.

Witton Park. Are these ironworkers or railway employees? The men are posed very erect with their shovels at arms.

Witton-le-Wear cricket team, in the early 1900s. The Lee brothers are at the back, third and fifth from the left.

Witton-le-Wear cricket team. They are pictured in 1909, with a trophy held by the young boy. On the back row, second from the left, is George Lee; front row, fourth from the left, is Ben Heslop and next to him, on the end, is Herbert Lee.

Witton-le-Wear football team. The team is seen in 1911. Ben Heslop is at the front left, with possibly one of the Lee brothers next to him.

North Bitchburn. The workforce at the local pipeyard are pictured in the early 1900s. Coal-fired circular kilns produced pipes, drainage equipment, junctions, bends and even garden jardinières (foreground), all with the familiar golden brown salt glaze.

Howden-le-Wear. The post office in High Street also doubled as the village grocer and provision merchant. In the windows Lingford's baking powder (a Bishop Auckland company) and Cadbury's cocoa are advertised. The post box slot is on the extreme left. Audrey Peacock is pictured with her mother here in the early 1930s.

Howden-le-Wear coaching club, in 1903. They pose outside the Green Tree Inn, where William Walburn was the licensee. Perhaps this was the 1900s equivalent of 'The Jolly Boys Outing'.

Fir Tree. Farming at the turn of the century, with the cheeky urchins still and composed for the photographer.

The blacksmith's shop at Fir Tree, c. 1900. William Hodgson was the blacksmith listed in Kelly's Directory of 1906.

Fir Tree cricket club. Winners of the South-West Durham Cricket League for the successive years 1921 and '22. From left to right, back row: G.W. Mawson, A.C. Parkin, T. Dunn, R. Patterson, I. Close, J.A. Close, T. Tomlinson, B.H. Cole, W. Close, M. Balmer (vice-president). Front: R. Balmer, W. Leybourne, J.W. Anderson (captain), The Finlay Roddam Cup, G. Simpson (vice-captain), H. Close, W. Braithwaite.

A group is pictured at Fir Tree drift mine, c. 1913. The coal was brought to the surface through a sloping or level tramway. Drift mines were often comparatively small and had short lives compared to deep mines with their vertical shafts.

Wolsingham. The ladies look very fetching in their costumes at the Women's Institute Victorian Dance in 1925.

Wolsingham. Willie Walton of Baxton Bank is the gentleman in the picture.

Frosterley School. In this 1926 group most of the girls are looking happy and most of the boys serious. Among the boys pictured are Sidney Boon (back row, second from the left) and John Dagg (on the extreme left). From left to right, the girls are: Mary Thompson, -?-, Esther Hall, Alice Reed, Hilda Spence (?), Gladys Watson, -?-, Annie Walton.

Frosterley Operatic Society, *c.* 1930.

Stanhope band, 1924. From left to right, back row: O. Forster, W. Walton, G. Pattinson, R. Pattinson, H. Storey, R. Calvert, A. Jacques. Middle row: J. Row (drum), M. Willis, J. Woodhall, J. Cleasby, H. Raine, C. Woodhall, W. Calvert, J. Forster. Front row: J. Allinson, G. Allinson, J. Pattinson, J. Wallace, -?-, J. Woodhall, J. Priestman, W. Hobson, ? Priestman. Seated at the front: G. Thompson, E. Pattinson.

Stanhope fossil tree. Found beside the Edmundbyers Road in 1914, this and at least one other were dug out of a quarry. Over 300 million years old, the decaying organic matter has been replaced by compressed sand.

Stanhope sanatorium staff. The Durham County Consumption Sanatorium for men was established in 1899 with forty-five beds.

Daddry Shield (also spelled Daddre). This Coronation procession of 22 June 1911 was photographed by Bee.

St John's Chapel. A group stands at the site of the old market cross which had been demolished in 1865. This postcard dates from the early 1900s and was published by Egglestone.

St John's Chapel. A whist drive and dance took place on 15 March 1912.

St John's Chapel. The national anthem is being sung in the Market Place on the Coronation Day of George V, 22 June 1911. (Photograph from J.W. Bee.)

St John's Chapel. Another procession is pictured on Coronation Day in 1911.

St John's Chapel. A soldiers outing towards the end of the First World War, for those who were convalescing from injuries or serious illness.

Westgate area. The workers in the field are taking a well earned rest and enjoying their 'bait'.

Boltsburn lead miners, *c.* 1905. Note the candle lamps and the sticks they used to aid walking underground.

Westgate. German prisoners of war are pictured in the snow in the Westgate area along with their British supervisors. POWs were employed as platelayers, labourers and boilermen on the railway at Rookhope as well as working in the quarries.

Westgate. More prisoners of war involved in quarry work. There were POW camps near Stanhope and at Harperley.

Westgate. A group of quarry workers are pictured about eighty years ago. The uniform flat caps worn were typical of northern industrial workers during the first half of this century.

Bollihope. Sheep shearing at Moor Rigg farm. This seems to be a happy group, with the young lady dressed perhaps in a male relative's uniform.

Bollihope. A family group are pictured in the garden, resting from their labours at Moor Rigg.

Westgate. John Dalkin is the blacksmith.

Lanehead, Cowshill. The Primitive Methodist chapel was built in 1843 and rebuilt in 1858, with 250 sittings. This vestry stone laying took place in the age of the postcard, so it is probably around 1900. There was a very good turnout for the ceremony.

Daddry Shield. This cheerful group of villagers, pictured around 1970, were celebrating winning the tidy village competition.

St John's Chapel. This group of people in the Wear are thought to be the Bee family, with Denise and Eva Peart.

The old Weardale band in 1866. Pictured at the Trevellers' Rest, Lanehead, from left to right, back row: Billy English, Milburn English, T. Pearson, J. Emerson, J. Peadon, T. Emerson, Jos Peart jnr. Front: John Watson, J. Hodgson, Joe Graham, W. James, W. Featherstone, J. English, Jos Peart.

Wellhope, Cowshill. This and the next few illustrations are of the Emerson family. John Emerson and his second wife, Tamar (?) Peart, on the occasion of his and her second marriage around 1884.

An Emerson wedding party. In the 1890s, one of John Emerson's three stepdaughters was married. Here they are on the way to her wedding with John Peart. Around the pony and trap are John's three sons, from the left; Fred, Tom and Joseph (who later became a successful optician in Newcastle and Sunderland).

Tom Emerson's marriage. A dale's society wedding around 1905, when Tom married Polly. He stayed in farming and died at Wellhope in 1938 at the comparatively early age of sixty.

Wedding. In 1935, Bessie, the only child of John Emerson's second marriage, married Sam Leslie at High House, Ireshopeburn.

In memoriam. A typical black-edged Victorian or Edwardian 'in memoriam' card, for Thomas Emerson, Whitestone House, Wellhope, Weardale. He died 3 March 1902, aged forty-eight. A check of the 1891 census returns showed many branches of the Emerson family at the head of Weardale, so it was not possible to confirm whether this gentleman was John Emerson's brother.

Wearhead. Re-opening of the Primitive Methodist church on 14 October 1911. This church originally opened in 1823. Methodism was a tremendous force in Weardale and John Wesley visited the dale thirteen times. At one time there were twenty-two chapels from Wolsingham westwards to the head of the dale.

Boltsburn. These wagons were derailed on Bolts Law incline, Rookhope in 1926. This trestle bridge across Bolts Burn was the scene of many incidents over the years. The children seem to be enjoying both the wreckage and the attention of the photographer.

Five

Industry and Commerce

Part Interior of Auckland Power Station.   The Cleveland and Durham County Power Company

Auckland power station. At the turn of the century electricity generation and distribution was in its infancy, and rested in the hands of small private companies and local authorities. The generators at the Cleveland and Durham County Power Company's station at Fylands Bridge, Bishop Auckland are pictured.

George Pit, Etherley. One of the old Etherley collieries of H. Stobart & Co. had been sunk in 1837 and provided work for many of the men of Escomb. The family, through Colonel Henry Stobart, was instrumental in building the Bishop Auckland & Weardale Railway. In County Durham in 1913 there were 304 collieries; now there are none.

Mine headgear at Wolfcleugh Mine, Rookhope. On the left is the narrow gauge railway down to Boltsburn and in the background is Groverake mine. Wolfcleugh was an old lead mine which was re-opened by the Weardale Lead Company in the early years of this century.

Boltsburn lead mine. In the background is the boiler house housing the equipment for working the air compressor and the steam winding engine. The boilers were coal fired with coal supplied initially via the Boltsburn incline, then by the aerial flight that ran down to Eastgate.

Slit Mine. This mine was situated halfway between Rookhope going in a south-westerly direction towards the River Wear. This shows the first stage in dressing ore. An enclosed waterwheel operated the crushing rollers and, through shafts and gearing, a small bank of mechanical jigs. This jig is basically a mechanized hotching tub in which the sieve is moved through eccentrics rather than a lever.

Stanner's Close steel works, Wolsingham. These works were founded by Charles Attwood in 1864 and passed into the hands of relatives, who traded as John Rogerson & Co., in 1885. At the turn of the century the company was the most important employer in Wolsingham and employed over 400 men.

Interior of Wolsingham steel works. This is a view of the gun shop. In W.M. Egglestone's book, *Picturesque Weardale*, of 1916, he indicated that the company had slotting, rifling, drilling, planing and various other machines, as well as band saws, lathes, cranes and endless other appliances, not forgetting their shearing machines and steam hammers, one of which had a six ton falling weight.

Wolsingham steel works. According to the hand-written caption on the back of this postcard it shows 'propeller brackets for HM battleships. Also some anchors with Mr Stobart, your uncle John. John Rogerson & Co. Ltd'. One of the most important customers in the years before the First World War was the Admiralty, to which steering gear and rudder frames were supplied. In addition, a six ton anchor was made for the famous ocean liner, *Mauretania*, which was launched on the Tyne by Swan Hunter & Wigham Richardson Ltd in 1906.

Brandon water wheel, Rookhope. This water wheel drove the water pumps in the lead mine. Behind the wheel are the lime kilns. This mine also produced 6oz of silver per ton of lead.

Smelt mill, Rookhope. The first mill was built here in 1752, but replaced some years later. Rebuilt in 1884, the new mill had five ore hearths, one slag hearth, a refining hearth and a roasting furnace.

Burnhope incline, Rookhope. A group of men pose on the railway line. Note the cable for hauling the wagons up the gradient.

Parsons Byers Quarry, near Frosterley. Locomotive *Aileen*, with Mr Banks on the footplate, Fenwick Smith (centre) and Joe Hayton, fireman, on the right. This locomotive had been built by Hawthorn Leslie in 1923, though when it arrived at Parsons Byers is not known. *Aileen* was still at the quarry in 1958, but only twelve months later all the locomotives had gone and the track had been dismantled.

Parsons Byers Quarry. The grabber helped to take some of the heavy labour out of quarrying.

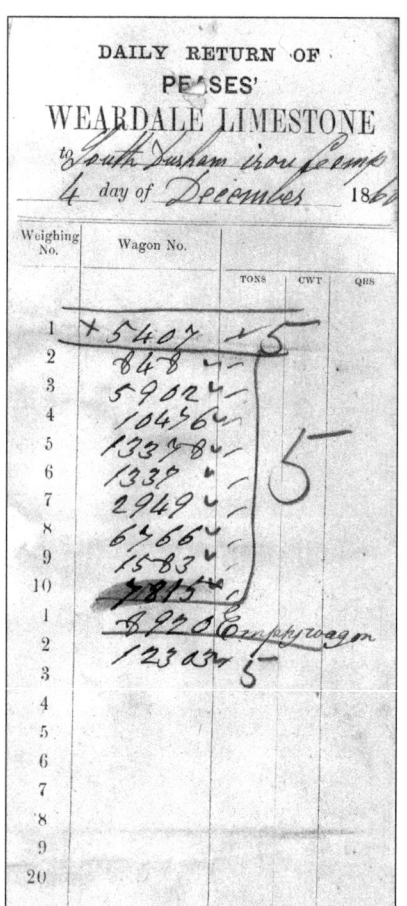

Stockton & Darlington Railway weigh bill. The S&DR sponsored and therefore controlled the Bishop Auckland & Weardale Railway. This bill shows a daily return of Peases' Weardale limestone sent to the South Durham Iron Co. on 4 December 1860.

Blast furnace, Stanhope Dene. This was erected in 1845 by Charles Attwood of the Weardale Iron Co. However, by the 1880s it had closed down. Stanhope Dene itself, at the western end of the town, was laid out in 1892 with footpaths, seats, bridges and a bandstand, by striking quarrymen in gratitude for the financial support they received from the townspeople.

RUINS OF FURNESS, Stanhope Dene

The Weardale District Highways Board steam roller and the road crew, Stanhope. In the background is the bridge connecting Stanhope Castle with its gardens.

Aeroplane in Stanhope Park. This was supposedly the first plane to land in Weardale, at the Stanhope Show in 1911.

Walter Willson's shop, Bishop Auckland. The shop, the supermarket of its era, was in South Road (now Newgate Street) in 1913. Note the cluttered appearance in the windows, the writing on the glass, and the meat hanging outside.

Bishop Auckland Industrial and Co-operative Society Ltd. The horse and cart advertises that excellence and quality from the bakery department is guaranteed.

Duff and Rowntree, Bishop Auckland. Situated at the head of Newgate Street leading into the Market Place, this building was in a prime position for sales. Duff and Rowntree, drapers, were operating in Bishop Auckland in the early 1900s, but had closed by 1938. The later tenants were W.E. Gill & Co., house furnishers.

Burton, tailor of taste, Bishop Auckland. Montague Burton, tailors, have had a shop here since at least 1938, at the corner of Newgate Street and Victoria Street.

Travelling kitchen, North Eastern Electric Supply Company Ltd. This travelling kitchen of the 1920s was used by NESCO, the forerunners of Northern Electric, to serve customers in the dales. In fact many rural areas did not receive mains electricity until the 1950s.

Blue Circle cement works, Eastgate. This was probably the best known landmark in the dale. Originally cement was sent out by rail, but from 1993 by road. Since the original publication of this book the works has closed and the plant demolished. There is currently an ambitious plan to turn the site into a leisure facility using thermal heat from deep underground.

Wolsingham post office. It is decorated for the Coronation of Edward VII in 1901. Michael Wharton was the postmaster around this time and his shop was in the Market Place. Note the large thermometer fastened to the wall on the left.

Ireshopeburn post office. Not as impressive as the building at Wolsingham, but still as important to the local people. Thomas Pentland was the postmaster in 1906. Perhaps this is him standing outside.

Burnhope reservoir. These two photographs show the reservoir development by the year 1925, three years after approval of the project to supply water to the steel and shipbuilding industries of Consett, South Shields and Sunderland.

Work stopped on building the reservoir because of the depression of 1926, but started again in 1929 as part of the Government's attempts to relieve unemployment.

Burnhope reservoir. The reservoir was finished in 1937, having submerged six farms at Burnhope hamlet in the process. On the left is the dam and valve control tower.

Burnhope reservoir, late 1930s. Nowadays, the spillway below the dam is grass covered and most of the reservoir is surrounded by woodland. Most of the dale's villages are supplied with water from Burnhope.

Tunstall reservoir. This reservoir is situated in Waskerley valley, two miles north of Wolsingham. It was brought into use in 1880 to supply water to the Ferryhill, Shildon, Spennymoor and Willington areas by means of a pipeline to North Beechburn. Wolsingham is also supplied from Tunstall.

Tunstall cottges. We see the road up from Wolsingham with, on the right, the overflow weir. The bungalows at the base of the dam were built for the use of workers at the reservoir. Egglestone, in his 1916 book, *Picturesque Weardale*, wrote that Tunstall 'is beautiful and worthy of a visit. The woods abound in wild birds, and rare flowers may be gathered in the plantation, and the angler may fish for trout'. The reservoir is as attractive today.

Witton Park ironworks. These four photographs show the derelict chimney and blast furnaces, and their demolition. The ironworks closed in 1884, but complete demolition of the remains did not take place until the 1930s.

One of six blast furnaces at Witton Park ironworks, in which cast iron was made by reducing ore with coke and adding limestone as a flux. The site chosen for the ironworks was known locally as Paradise!

Blowing up the blast furnaces at Witton Park ironworks.

It is apparent here how close the ironworks were to public buildings, though they may also have been derelict.

Six

Buildings – Spiritual and Temporal

High House chapel, Ireshopeburn. This is the second oldest Methodist chapel in continuous use in the country, and was founded in 1760. The building was enlarged in 1872 and restored in 1984. John Wesley preached both in the chapel and on several occasions outside, nearby, beside a thorn bush. The adjoining former manse now houses the Weardale Museum.

The Guest House, West, St. John's Chapel. 11879

The Guest House, Ireshopeburn. Originally this was a school called New House, which was built with subscriptions from mine owners in 1854. At one time it housed over 200 boys and girls. By 1882 the school had closed and initially it became a residential property. However, by 1938 it had become the Weardale Guest House and was run by Mrs J. Rowell. The postcard, a 1930s view, incorrectly states that the house was in St John's Chapel. Nowadays, it is The Weardale Inn and provides parking for visitors to the adjacent Weardale Museum.

WESLEYAN. CHAPEL. WESTGATE.

Wesleyan chapel, Westgate. This chapel was built in 1791 and enlarged in 1890. Methodism made a tremendous impact in upper Weardale and this resulted in the great spread of chapel building to replace the small societies which had been meeting in cottages and barns.

108

Methodist church, Westgate. The split between Wesleyans and (Primitive) Methodists over doctrine in the early nineteenth century resulted in many villages having two churches or chapels. The Primitive Methodist church was built in 1870 with seating for 700.

All Saints church, Eastgate. This established church was erected in 1888, being financially supported by J.R.W. Hildyard of Horsley Hall. He was the local JP and principal local landowner.

Stanhope Castle. The present building was constructed in 1798 for Cuthbert Rippon MP. Alterations were made in 1875 by Henry Pease who added a new entrance from the Market Place. Since then the castle has changed hands many times, from the Church Commissioners, to an approved school and finally to private apartments.

Gardens, Stanhope Castle, c. 1913. This shows the gardens, which were across a road and were connected to the castle by a single-arched stone bridge (see page 97). Cuthbert Rippon jnr laid out paths, fruit, flower and vegetable gardens as well as greenhouses.

The gantry, Stanhope Sanatorium. The consumption sanatorium was established in 1899 and originally had forty-five beds. Fresh air for TB patients was considered essential.

The huts, Stanhope Sanatorium. The fresh air idea is clearly being put into practice!

New Town Hotel, Stanhope. This house was originally the residence of the Roddam family who were Justices of the Peace, landowners and estate agents from the late nineteenth century well into the twentieth. However, by this time, the 1930s, the house had been converted into a hotel.

Church of St Thomas and War Memorial, Stanhope. This little 'cathedral' of the dale was built in the twelfth century and was restored in the nineteenth. Due to its annual revenue of £5,000 from the lead mines, the living at Stanhope, of £1,650, was one of the richest in England, and attracted a succession of socially well connected priests, many of whom rose to higher office later – three in the last century became bishops. The war memorial is situated in the churchyard wall, along with a fossil sandstone tree, to the left (not visible in the picture).

Frosterley church. St Michael's church, with its fine spire was opened in 1869. Contrast the living of the vicar at the turn of the century – of £400 – with that at Stanhope.

Redgate Hall, Wolsingham. This was situated off the road from Wolsingham to Tow Law. Cuthbert Bainbridge, a member of the well known Newcastle department store-owning family, who originated in Weardale, lived here for a while in the 1860s.

Bay Horse Hotel, Wolsingham. This view shows the hotel in flames in 1916, when a fire partially destroyed it. However, the blaze didn't catch the photographer nor the watching crowd unawares. There was plenty of action to watch and record, with the fire fighters looking very efficient on the ladder.

Bay Horse Hotel, Wolsingham. This view, in calmer times, is probably from around 1907 when Amos Stephen Hunt was in charge. The writing on the second bay window from the left reads 'Smoke Room'. Appropriate, given the previous picture! The Bay Horse Hotel is still open today.

Bradley Hall, Wolsingham. The hall is located about two miles east of Wolsingham on the main road up the dale. This was originally a fortified farmhouse in the fifteenth century and there has been a building on this site dating back as far as the twelfth century. The hall had started to decay by 1800 and here we see it in the early years of this century. Today it is under the protection of English Heritage who carried out urgent repairs in 1995.

Fawnlees, Wolsingham. This hall is north west of Wolsingham, near Thornhope Beck, and was mentioned in a bishop's estates survey in the fourteenth century. The façade pictured dates from the eighteenth century. Tenants over the years have included George D. Wooler JP in 1856 and Hugh L. Mackay in 1938.

Pavilion 1, Holywood Hall, Wolsingham. This hall was built by Charles Attwood, the steel magnate, in 1864, and stands on the east bank of Waskerley Beck, north of Wolsingham. In 1905 it was bought by Durham County Council with a view to converting it into a sanatorium with 100 beds.

Holywood Hall, Wolsingham in the 1930s. The medical superintendent and matron are pictured at the main entrance of the hall. The first step in curing consumption or TB was thought to be providing a clean environment, pure air and clean food. Holywood Hall has since been converted into a number of separate dwellings.

Grammar school, Wolsingham. The grammar school, originally in Church Lane, was founded in 1613, though the building shown here was opened in 1911 at the western end of the town. This building is still in use, though the railings have been replaced by hedges, and trees now partially shelter the front and sides.

Wesleyan chapel, Wolsingham. This chapel, built in the Gothic style and seating 300, was opened in 1862, replacing a smaller building that stood behind and to the left of the view shown.

Parish church, Wolsingham. This church, of St Mary and St Stephen, was erected on the site of a Norman church dating from 1180. The adapted and expanded church was virtually rebuilt in 1848/49, though the original Norman tower was retained. It is claimed that the churchyard has one of the finest collection of tombstones in the country, including that of Charles Attwood.

Parish Church, Wolsingham. 3881

Hamsterley Church.

Hamsterley church. The church of St James was founded in 1180 and finally restored in 1884/85. The church is about 1,200 metres east of the village, towards Witton Bridge over the Wear. The poison victim, Mary Jane Dodds, is buried here.

Hoppyland Park, Hamsterley. This lies nearly a mile north west of Bedburn, on the edge of Hamsterley Forest. This was the seat of the Leaton-Blenkinsopp family in the nineteenth and early twentieth century, but by 1938 the incumbent was Colonel Thomas Dowling.

Methodist chapel and the church, Witton Park. The church is St Paul's and was built in 1877 when the local ironworks was still operating and there was a necessity, said the vicar of Escomb, for 'making some better provision for the spiritual wants of Witton Park in this parish'. The Primitive Methodist chapel had been built around 1850, and was rebuilt in 1883 as shown here. Witton Park and Escomb had increased in population from 510 in 1841 to 4,313 in 1871, but then reduced to 3,401 by 1891. Their spiritual needs were great and the village boasted seven churches and chapels at one time.

Witton-le-Wear church. The church of St Philip and St James has been on the site since Saxon times, but the Norman church, which was here from the twelfth century, was in such a state of decay by the end of the nineteenth century, that it was rebuilt and re-consecrated in 1902. The Norman south door and thirteenth-century north arcade were re-used in the reconstruction.

Primitive Methodist chapel, Witton-le-Wear. This is another village which housed chapels of both the Wesleyan and Primitive factions of the Methodist Movement. This chapel was built in 1850 as 'Rohabath Primitive Methodist Chapel'.

Old Wesleyan church, Etherley. Some of the small churches looked rather similar to ordinary private dwellings, such as the one shown here. Indeed the police had a station on the ground floor. This is a centenary view, from seventy years ago, of the building which was erected in 1829 and enlarged in 1840.

VA hospital, Etherley. This is thought to be the fever hospital that was situated in Tindale Crescent, Bishop Auckland. When epidemics of such illnesses as scarlet fever and diphtheria occurred, the patients were sent to isolation hospitals such as this, and their homes were fumigated. My father and aunt were sent to this hospital when they contracted scarlet fever around 1930. The hospital was always known as the 'fever' hospital.

Smelt House, Howden-le-Wear. This house was named after the area where slag and cinders had been found, suggesting that iron had been smelted in the distant past. The house was rebuilt in about 1850 in the Elizabethan style and the grounds were laid out ornamentally by George Coates. The house was owned by Mrs Fryer in 1906 and Edward Shaw-Carew in 1938.

South Lodge, Etherley. This is the southern entrance to the Witton Castle estate.

Witton Castle. A manor house was built here in the twelfth century, but the foundations of the present building were laid down by Ralph de Eure early in the fifteenth century. He had received permission from the Bishop of Durham to fortify his manor house. Over the years the castle has changed ownership many times, with the Chaytor family owning the estate through the nineteenth century and well into the twentieth. It is now owned by the Lambton family.

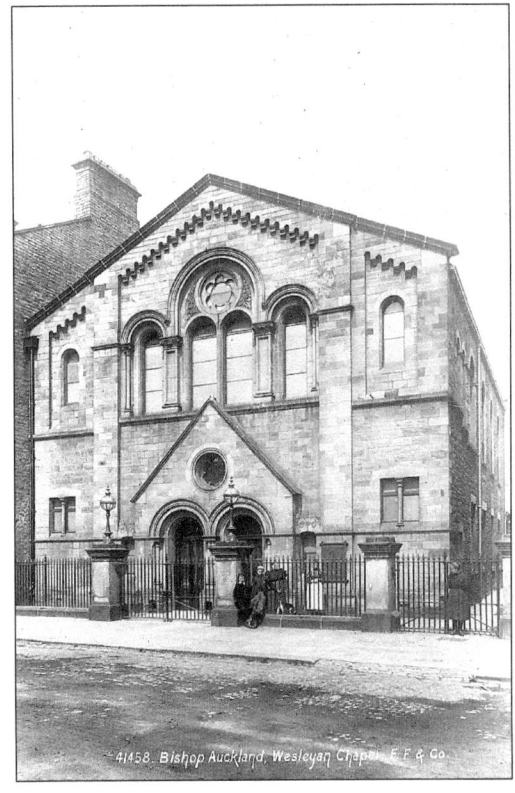

Wesleyan chapel, North Bondgate, Bishop Auckland. This was rebuilt a second time in 1866 to replace previous chapels of 1804 and 1842. It was itself replaced by a larger Wesleyan church in Newgate Street in 1914.

Escomb Saxon church. This celebrated church was built sometime between 670 and 690, using stones from the Roman Fort at Vinovia. The building is simple, tall and narrow with irregular windows and stonework. The stones in the upper three feet are smaller than those lower down. The church was restored between 1875 and 1880.

Inside Escomb church. Interesting features include sundials, Saxon crosses and windows, Roman inscriptions and the chancel arch.

Auckland Castle, from the High Plains, dating from before 1930. The rich and powerful Prince Bishops of the Palatinate of Durham lived as princes rather than bishops. Of their many country seats, the one at Auckland, overlooking the Rivers Wear and Gaunless, is the only one to remain.

Chapel and grounds, Auckland Castle. The chapel of St Peter was built in the twelfth century as a banqueting hall and was converted for use as a chapel in 1665.

Entrance hall, Auckland Castle. Known originally as the gentlemen's hall, this is believed to be the oldest part of the old manor house, linking the twelfth-century great hall to the servants' quarters.

Drawing room, Auckland Castle. Also called the throne room this houses numerous portraits of past bishops. The bishop's throne is at the far end.

Dining room, Auckland Castle. This part of the castle was added in the sixteenth century. Thirteen unique paintings by the Spanish artist, Francesco Zurburan are hung on the walls.

THE CHAPEL, BISHOP AUCKLAND CASTLE.

Chapel, Auckland Castle. Restoration work in the chapel was undertaken in 1828, 1888 and between 1978 and 1983. Latterly work was required in respect of erosion, wood beetles and dry rot, stonework, damp-proofing and drainage. The chapel organ and organ gallery were also renovated. The chapel is illuminated by stained-glass windows, illustrating the founding of Christianity in the north-east.

Farewell. I am thinking of you at Bishop Auckland. This postcard, sent in 1912, seems appropriate as the last entry in this journey up and down Weardale.